CARING FOR THE PLANET
RIVERS AND WETLANDS

Neil Champion

A⁺
Smart Apple Media

Published by Smart Apple Media
2140 Howard Drive West, North Mankato, MN 56003

Design and production by Helen James

Photographs by Alamy (Bill Bachman, blickwinkel, David Hoffman Photo
Library, Rod Edwards, eWildz, eye35.com, James Gritz, Holt Studios
International Ltd, Chris Howes / Wild Places Photography, ImageState,
James Davis Photography, Jon Arnold Images, Byron Jorjorian, Jason
Lindsey, Roland Liptak, John Morgan, nagelestock.com, Wolfgang Pölzer,
Fredrik Renander, GEORGE AND MONSERRATE SCHWARTZ, ALIKI SAPOUNTZI
/ aliki image library, Paul Springett, Steve Bloom Images, Keren Su / China
Span, David South, Tom Till, Norman Tomalin, Vstock, Wildscape)

Library of Congress Cataloging-in-Publication Data

Champion, Neil.
Rivers and wetlands / by Neil Champion.
p. cm. — (Caring for the planet)
ISBN-13: 978-1-58340-510-9
1. Rivers—Juvenile literature. 2. Steam ecology—Juvenile literature. 3.
Wetlands—Juvenile literature. 4. Wetland ecology—Juvenile literature. I.
Title. II. Series.

QH97.C48 2005
577.64—dc22   2004052516

First Edition

9 8 7 6 5 4 3 2 1

Contents

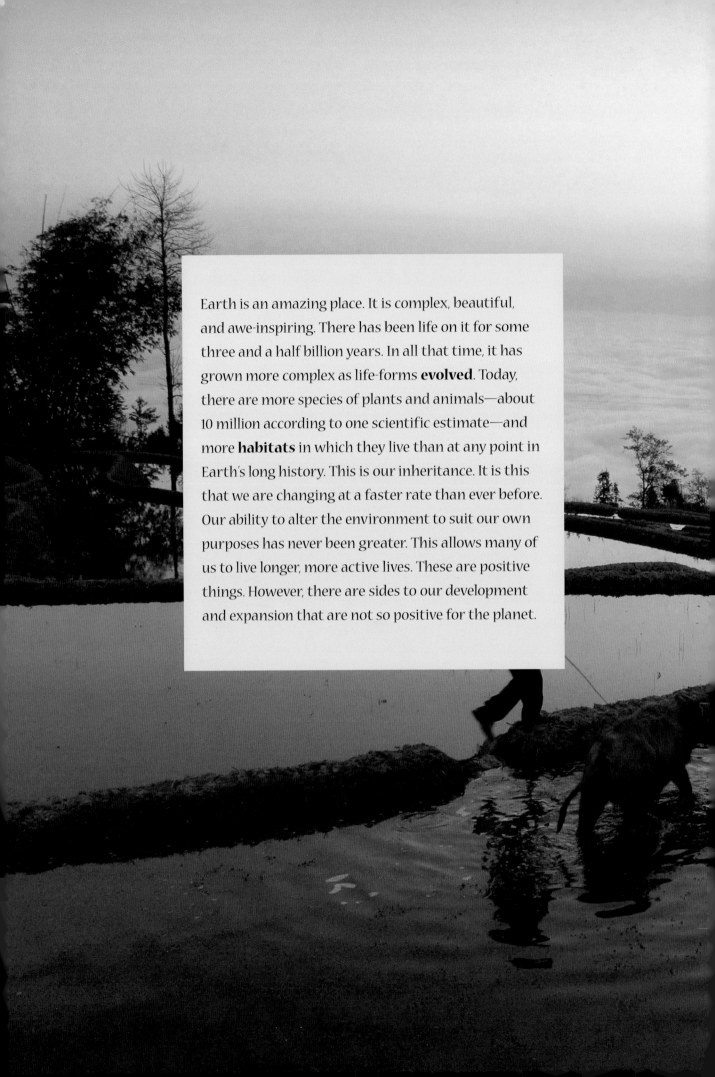

Earth is an amazing place. It is complex, beautiful, and awe-inspiring. There has been life on it for some three and a half billion years. In all that time, it has grown more complex as life-forms **evolved**. Today, there are more species of plants and animals—about 10 million according to one scientific estimate—and more **habitats** in which they live than at any point in Earth's long history. This is our inheritance. It is this that we are changing at a faster rate than ever before. Our ability to alter the environment to suit our own purposes has never been greater. This allows many of us to live longer, more active lives. These are positive things. However, there are sides to our development and expansion that are not so positive for the planet.

The River and Wetland Biome

Environmental scientists divide the world up into large natural zones called biomes. These biomes include rivers and wetlands, deserts, **temperate** woodlands, rain forests, **tundra**, grasslands or prairies, and oceans. Each biome has a certain type of climate and is characterized by its plant and animal life, which is adapted to live in the conditions it offers.

This book looks at life in the river and wetland biome and the threats rivers and wetlands face today. It also looks at some solutions to these threats that may protect what is left of the natural world.

What Are Wetlands?

Lakes, marshes, fens, bogs, swamps, floodplains, coastal regions, and **estuaries** are all types of wetlands. What they all have in common is a mixture of land and water. As the name implies, these habitats are very wet much of the time. They often go through cycles of flooding and dry periods.

All of the plants and animals that live in wetlands have evolved to live in landscapes that are sometimes water, sometimes land, and usually a very rich combination of the two. Some plants and animals can tolerate certain amounts of salty water; others cannot. Some need rich soils in which to flourish, whereas others can live in infertile and acidic bogs.

Problems occur in wetlands when change is brought about by human intervention. Problems may be caused when people flood the landscape through the building of dams, drain the land of its natural water, make salty water less salty, or make fresh water more salty. Plants and animals can often adapt, but they need lots of time to do so. People often change the environment very quickly to suit their own needs—for example, by removing water from a river to use in homes or industries.

Wetlands are not productive in human terms; people cannot easily find an economic use for them. This has been their downfall in some places. People have wanted to change them in order to farm the land or build

on it. In warm parts of the world, wetlands are breeding grounds for mosquitoes. These small insects can carry malaria, a disease that causes a life-threatening fever. It is estimated that about 200 million people worldwide have the disease. Drying out the habitat so that mosquitoes cannot breed and spread the disease might seem like a good idea, but wetlands are then lost.

What Makes a Wetland?

There are many types of wetlands around the world. However, they all have certain qualities in common. Wetlands require soils that hold on to water and provide some nutrients for plants, as well as a climate with lots of rainfall or the availability of water from some other source. The flooding cycle in a wetland can be daily, as in the case of tidal estuaries; the sea comes in and floods, then goes back out to expose the land again. Or the cycle can be yearly, with **monsoon** rains providing floods that are then followed by months of dryness. During times of flooding, the soil becomes saturated, or waterlogged.

Everglades

The Everglades National Park in Florida, one of the best-known wetland habitats. It has World Heritage status in recognition of its international importance.

Wetland Definitions

Although wetlands can all be broadly defined together, they do come in a variety of distinct habitats, depending upon the mix of soil, amount of water, altitude, and vegetation. Here are some of the more common wetlands found around the world:

*Swamps are areas of land that remain underwater year-round. They are characterized by trees and shrubs that grow out of the wet, fertile soils. They are generally rich in wildlife—plants, birds, and fish, as well as crocodiles and alligators.

*Marshes are lowland wetlands characterized by nutrient-rich soils. They are fed by local streams and runoff from precipitation that washes nutrients into them. This in turn allows plants, such as rushes and reeds, to thrive, along with bird, fish, and amphibian communities. Coastal salt marshes are affected by tides, and plants and animals there have adapted to the salty environment.

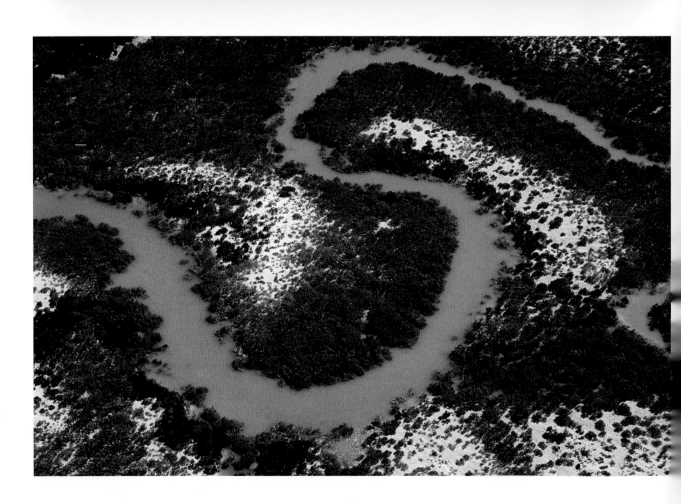

English Fens

The fenland landscape of Cambridgeshire in England. Drainage canals and ditches have created an artificial landscape in which cereal crops can be grown.

Australian Creek

This river meanders through the landscape close to the coast in Australia. When the tide comes in, its waters mix with the sea, creating a special type of river environment (opposite page).

*Bogs are characterized by lots of spongy peat and acidic soils in which only a few specialized plants and animals can live. Bogs get their water from precipitation rather than local streams. This has the effect of washing nutrients out of the soil rather than delivering them.

*Fens are peaty lowland wetlands that get plenty of nutrients from the surrounding landscape through the drainage of water. Therefore, they are less acidic than bogs and have more diverse plants and animals living among them. They are characterized by lots of grasses and reeds growing out of their standing waters, with wildflowers around the edges.

Wading Bird

The great white egret or heron, a bird that wades in shallow wetland habitats, spears fish and frogs with its sharp bill.

The timing of floodwaters is crucial to the existence of wetlands. This is because the plants and animals that depend on wetlands for survival have adapted to the cycle of flooding. Migrating birds, breeding frogs, flowering water lilies, and **spawning** fish all depend on a regular natural flood cycle. Even human communities that have developed alongside annually flooding rivers, such as the Nile, or floodplains, such as those found in Bangladesh, rely on a regular pattern of flooding.

Fertility and Infertility

Some wetlands have a very low fertility. Bogs are one example. They develop where there is lots of rainfall—in the mountains of North Wales, Scotland, and Ireland, for example. Here, the soil is acidic and has very few nutrients. Not many plants or animals can survive in such an environment. Among the few life-forms are **mosses**, cotton grass, and strange plants such as the sundew, pitcher plant, and butterwort, which supplement their diets by digesting insects that they catch on their sticky leaves. The water

10

that collects in bogs is mostly stagnant, which means that it is still water, not moving like the water in a stream or river. **Algae** grow on it and take oxygen out of the water, and the resulting lack of oxygen makes it very difficult for other plants to grow. Sphagnum moss is one plant that can cope with the conditions of acidity and compete with the algae. This moss is like a sponge. It can hold up to 15 times its own weight in water, which is useful in times of low rainfall.

Other types of wetlands are far more productive. Fens, for example, provide a much richer environment for plants and animals. Fens are similar to bogs but occur at lower altitudes. They have more nutrients in the soil due to better movement of water and the collection of nutrients from the surrounding rocks and **sediment**. Lakes and ponds also enable a wide array of birds, fish, trees, and water-loving plants to thrive.

Lake Algae
Algae growing on the edge of a salty lake in Colorado. When water evaporates, minerals washed into a landlocked lake can become very concentrated.

Where Are Wetlands?

Wetlands are found on all of the continents of Earth except Antarctica. They cover just over five percent of the planet's surface. Some wetlands are cold, such as those found on the tundra of Siberia, and others are warm, such as those found in countries on or near the equator. Wetlands vary enormously. The climate, soil, water, and vegetation all influence how any particular wetland looks and which animals and plants live there. Some of the most famous wetland areas include:

The Everglades, Florida

This site in southern Florida covers more than one and a half million acres (607,000 ha) and is made up of swampland, mangrove forests, salt marshes, and extensive freshwater lakes with tropical hardwood forests. The Everglades is well known for its plant and animal life. Many birds nest here or use the area as a resting place on their migration routes. It is one of the wildest regions of the United States, and the only people who live in its depths are the Seminoles, a tribe of Native Americans.

The Everglades helps protect the surrounding region from flood damage and also provides free and natural water filtration to the citizens of Florida. Due to its high profile, the Everglades also performs a role in educating the public about wetland habitats and the **ecology** of wild areas. Many schools and colleges visit the region to study it.

The Sundarbans, Bangladesh

The Sundarbans covers almost one and a half million acres (607,000 ha). It is found where the great rivers of the Ganges and Brahmaputra meet and run into the Bay of Bengal. It is very important for many reasons. It is rich in wildlife and plants, and is home to the Royal Bengal tiger—an endangered species. Other endangered animals that live in its midst include the Pallas fishing eagle and the river terrapin. The Sundarbans makes up the biggest mangrove forest in the world and protects the landscape from devastating monsoon winds and the huge tidal waves that seasonally pound the shores of Bangladesh.

The Tanguar Haor, Bangladesh

Bangladesh has another internationally important wetland site: the Tanguar Haor. This freshwater wetland is located in the northeastern part of the country on the floodplain of the Surma River. It is a swamp in which forests grow, and it is home to more than 100 types of fish and 200 types of birds, many of them important waterfowl. Ten of these bird species are endangered.

Threatened Species

A tiger swimming across a river in India. These magnificent animals have been hunted to near-extinction and are today protected by international law.

The Okavango Delta, Botswana

This enormous inland **delta** is found on the border of Botswana and Namibia. It is an area of extensive swampland fed by the Okavango River and is known as the jewel of the Kalahari, as it is a huge, wet **oasis** in the middle of a dry landscape. The 17-million-acre (6.9 million ha) delta gets flooded on an annual basis, when the land disappears underwater, reemerging as the water subsides. It is home to many important fish, bird, insect, and mammal species.

Point Calimere Wildlife and Bird Sanctuary, India

Although the Point Calimere region is small—95,000 acres (38,500 ha)—in comparison with some other wetlands, it is an important area for wildlife, especially birds. The gray pelican and the flamingo are just two magnificent species that live here. The Point Calimere region is situated on the far southeastern coast of India facing the Indian Ocean. It is made up of shallow water and **lagoons** along the shoreline, as well as mangrove swamps.

Okavango Delta

A sea eagle snatching a fish from the waters of the Okavango, the world's largest inland delta, on the edge of the Kalahari Desert in Africa.

Rannoch Moor, Scotland

Rannoch Moor is another small wetland, at 3,700 acres (1,500 ha). It is typical of the upland blanket bogs found in Britain—areas poor in nutrients, with acidic lakes and stagnant water. Rare and very specialized plants live here, and it is an important breeding ground for wetland birds.

Small but Significant

At almost 131,300 square miles (340,000 sq km), Finland is a relatively small country—smaller than the state of California—in northeastern Europe. It shares a border with Russia, and one-third of its territory is inside the Arctic Circle. It has the highest proportion of wetlands of any country in Europe, with more than 60,000 lakes. It is also one of the most ecologically active nations, and the wetlands of Finland are very well protected. Not only do the Finns care about their own landscape; they are very active in helping to protect wetlands in Third World countries as well. Finland is an example of how small nations can effectively protect the environment if the people and government have the will to act.

Icy Loch

Ice sometimes forms on the reeds growing out of the acidic, stagnant waters of Rannoch Moor in the Highlands of Scotland.

Why Are Wetlands Important?

Wetlands are important for many reasons. They are home to abundant vegetation and wildlife, much of which could not live in any other habitat. Scientists consider biodiversity to be important in the natural world because it provides a rich variety of animal and plant types. To support this biodiversity, there need to be plenty of different types of habitats in which animals and plants can live. Wetlands provide one such habitat. They also provide a home and resources for several human communities. In addition, wetlands serve as natural water filters, help prevent erosion and floods by soaking up excess water in times of heavy rain, and help keep carbon dioxide out of the atmosphere.

Wildlife Paradise or Wasteland?

In recent times, people in many parts of the world have seen wetlands as wastelands. So they have drained them and turned them into farmland or land on which to build houses. In truth, many wetlands are very fertile places. A great variety of specialized plants such as mangrove trees, reeds, bulrushes, cotton grasses, and water-loving plants live there, as do insects such as dragonflies; birds such as curlews, oystercatchers, and ducks; reptiles such as alligators, crocodiles, and snakes; and large mammals such as water buffaloes.

Wetland Plants

Scientists have divided the plants that grow in wetlands into three basic types. Some plants grow on the banks of rivers, lakes, and other wetlands; they like it wet, but not too wet. Floating plants grow on the surface of lakes and slow-moving rivers. They have broad leaves to help them do this. One example is the giant lily, an Amazon plant with a leaf that can measure five feet (1.5 m) across. The third type of wetland plants grows underwater. The mangrove tree, which is found in tropical regions along coasts and in river estuaries, is one example. These trees have adapted to the salty conditions and floodwaters of these regions. Their bark is waterproof and able to keep out wood-boring worms that would eventually kill other types of trees. Mangroves make good homes for fish and shellfish, which can hide among their roots.

Australian Mangroves

A mangrove swamp in the Northern Territory of Australia. The trees grow straight out of the water and have adapted to these conditions.

Rice

Rice is a special form of an ancient wetland grass. It has been developed by people over thousands of years to become one of the most important types of food on Earth. Today, rice makes up a major part of the diet of more than half of the human race. It is grown in flooded fields, known as paddies, in more than 100 hot and wet countries around the world, including Japan, China, Thailand, the Philippines, Indonesia, and India.

Endangered Animals and Wetlands

Wetlands provide homes for many animals, including several that are in danger of extinction due to habitat loss. Endangered animals of worldwide importance that live in wetlands and rivers include:

• The Royal Bengal tiger, which has been hunted to near extinction. More than 600 of these magnificent big cats live in the Sundarbans wetland in India and Bangladesh.

River Reptiles

The gavial and its close relative, the false gavial, live in rivers feeding on fish and frogs. They are reptiles and members of the crocodile family.

• The gavial, a large relative of the crocodile reaching up to 23 feet (7 m) long, which lives in the rivers of northern India. It has been hunted for its leathery skin and has suffered due to the loss of its wetland habitat.

• Freshwater dolphins, of which there are five different types worldwide. The baiji dolphin lives in the Yangtze River in China. There are thought to be only 200 or 300 left.

• The European otter, which has become extinct in many European countries, mostly due to farmers' use of some **insecticides**. Even when the worst offender, a chemical called dieldrin, was banned, the loss of habitat and pollution of rivers meant that the otter population did not rebound.

• The Siberian crane, a beautiful bird found in China and Russia. Its story is familiar—it was hunted, its rivers and lakes were polluted, and the wetlands where it bred were drained.

European Otters

The European otter is making a comeback in Britain as waterways are made less polluted and conservation projects restore its river habitat.

The IUCN Red Book

*The International Union for the Conservation of Nature (IUCN), once known as the World Conservation Union, was set up by the United Nations in 1948. It is based in Switzerland, with the goal of promoting **sustainable** development throughout the world and protecting habitats and the plants and animals that live in them. It keeps a record of endangered species worldwide, called* The Red Book. *Scientists and environmentalists can use the information in this book to protect wildlife in their country. The book, which is available to anyone, is one of the most useful sources of information on the state of conservation in the world.*

Wetlands and Traditional People

Wetlands all around the world have traditionally played a major role in the lives of local people. Communities as far apart and diverse as the Marsh Arabs in Iraq, the Turkana people of Kenya, and native peoples of Australia all harvest rivers and wetlands for food and even materials with which to build homes. The people on the shores of Lake Titicaca high in the mountains of South America, for example, make boats out of reeds to travel on this huge expanse of water. The Kenyans who live on the shores of Lake Turkana use the reeds that grow in the water to make their homes and live off the fish in the lake. Their impact on the natural environment is very small. Communities like these have existed for thousands of years, taking what they need from the environment but not damaging the things they touch. However, in today's world of big business, traditional peoples have been **marginalized**. They often do not have a voice when it comes to the future of the landscape that sustains them.

Natural Filters

Besides providing a home for plants, animals, and people, wetlands provide a natural cleaning service, helping to filter out harmful chemicals and decomposing matter from the water. This is done in two ways: through sediment, which acts like a sieve to catch pollutants, and through certain plants that catch harmful chemicals. The water hyacinth is one such plant. It grows in

swamps and lakes and makes water purer by absorbing chemicals and **neutralizing** them. Wetlands also purify rivers and help keep them flowing by allowing sediment to settle, removing it from the river water. This water-cleaning benefit is so important that some governments around the world are encouraging people to restore wetlands. This can save them money in the long run, as it has been estimated that just two and a half acres (1 ha) of wetland can do the job of an expensive man-made water treatment facility.

Fighting Erosion

Another major role of wetlands is that of protector of the landscape. The plants that grow in and around the water help to bind together the sediment and soils and prevent erosion. In coastal regions around the world, this protection is vital to human communities. Vegetation helps maintain the structure of shoreline defenses—for example, grasses hold together protective sand dunes—against the daily impact of the waves that pound against them. In places such as the Sundarbans in India and

South American Lake

People navigating the waters of Lake Titicaca in traditional reed boats. This is the largest freshwater lake in South America and—at an altitude of 12,000 feet (3,820 m)— one of the highest.

Monsoon Floods

Monsoon conditions in Varanasi, a city in northern India on the banks of the Ganges River. The effects of this seasonal event can be made worse by human actions, such as the removal of tree cover from the surrounding hillsides.

Bangladesh, where in times of storm waves can be more than 13 feet (4 m) high, the mangrove forests that grow along the coast help protect human lives, as well as farms and homes. This defense line is so important that the Bangladeshi government has spent money to plant additional mangrove trees.

Flood Prevention

Wetlands also help regulate the flow of rivers. They do this by moderating the effects of heavy rain and floods and by allowing water to flow even in times of drought. Wetlands act like huge sponges. Rivers that flow through a wetland area carry lots of water during times of heavy rain. Without the presence of the wetland, this water would spill over the land and could flood nearby cities and towns. Fens, bogs, and swamps all help soak up the excess water, preventing flooding or lessening the severity of a flood. In times of little water in the dry season, the excess water that the sponge-like wetland has absorbed continues to supply the river system with a certain amount of water due to slow seepage.

Farmers and communities can still get water even when it has not rained for some time. The construction of dams for making **hydroelectric power** and the diversion of rivers for **irrigation** pose serious threats to this natural function of wetlands.

The Lungs of the World

Peat bogs, formed out of decaying plant and tree matter in bogs and fens over thousands of years, play a role in helping keep the gases in our atmosphere healthy for people and animals to breathe. They have been called part of the "lungs" of the world. Peat bogs lock up **carbon** in the form of decomposing vegetation. Scientists have estimated that there are about 888,000 square miles (2.3 million sq km) of peat bog in the world today. This means there is a lot of carbon kept out of the atmosphere— about 550 billion tons (500 billion t) of carbon trapped in the dead organic matter that makes up peat bogs. This is important, since carbon dioxide, which is formed when carbon combines with oxygen, is one of the main **greenhouse gases** thought to contribute to **global warming**. There is already too much of this gas in the atmosphere. It is therefore important to keep the peat bogs around the world as they are, locking up these reserves of carbon, rather than burning them as fuel and releasing carbon dioxide into the air.

Peat Bogs

Peat bogs stretching out toward mountains in the Highlands of Scotland. This type of bog is found in cold temperate zones in the northern hemisphere.

Rivers of the World

There are some amazing natural scenes to be found along
the mighty rivers of the world. On the U.S.-Canada border, the
tremendous roar of Niagara Falls deafens all who come to witness
the 167-foot (50 m) plunge of the Niagara River. The Zaire River, the
second largest in Africa after the Nile River, contains more than 100
miles (160 km) of some of the most dangerous rapids in the world,
including a gorge called the Gates of Hell. The Amazon, perhaps
the most famous river of them all, runs for more than 4,040 miles
(6,500 km) and carries more water than any other river. It enters
the Atlantic Ocean on the equator at an estuary that is 50 miles (80
km) wide. The river pushes out so much water that fresh water can
still be tasted on the surface of the salty ocean more than 37 miles
(60 km) out to sea. The Ganges is one of the most revered rivers
in the world. It flows through India and Bangladesh and is sacred
to millions of Hindus. In Europe, the Danube flows through many
countries from its source in the Black Forest of Germany to its
delta in Romania on the shores of the Black Sea. Its waters provide
sustenance to important capital cities such as Vienna, Austria, and
Budapest, Hungary.

All rivers, great and small, are sources of life. They are part of the
huge and complex natural process that moves water around the
world from one place to another: the **water cycle**. Rivers develop
in high places such as hills and mountains, which get more rainfall

than the surrounding lowlands. Gravity ensures that rivers always run downhill, toward the sea, where most rivers end. As a river flows downhill, it gathers more water from rainfall and from streams that feed into it. When it reaches flatter land, it slows down and meanders toward the sea or a large lake.

Niagara Falls

The Niagara Falls in the northeastern U.S. The Niagara River plunges more than 150 feet (50 m), forming one of the most powerful waterfalls in the world.

Rivers and Settlements

All early human settlements grew up alongside rivers. Fresh water for drinking and washing is essential to human survival, and rivers provided this. Rivers also provided a very different way of getting around—by boat. Trade is a key part of human existence, and rivers gave early communities convenient highways.

The big rivers of Africa and Asia—including the Tigris, Euphrates, Ganges, Mekong, and Nile—helped human settlements develop into large, flourishing civilizations thousands of years ago. The floodplains along their banks allowed people to grow vast quantities of food and to graze their cattle on lush grasses. For example, the great kingdoms of ancient Egypt sprang up 5,000 years ago on the banks of the world's longest river, the Nile, whose annual floods poured rich, muddy sediment full of nutrients onto what would otherwise be barren desert sands. This allowed

What Is a Floodplain?

Floodplains are areas of land that run alongside rivers. In times of heavy rain or melting snows, rivers often flood their banks. When this happens, floodplains are covered by water. The economies of some areas rely on the rich sediment that washes over the land when these floods occur. This adds fertility to the soil. Farmers look forward to such floods, recognizing that their crops and livelihood depend on them. The Niger River, which flows through Mali in West Africa, for example, has floodplains that allow a large population of people to live in what otherwise would be a barren landscape.

Floodplains are threatened when dams are built, rivers are diverted, and people take water for their crops higher up the river. Often built to provide hydroelectric power for towns and cities, dams reduce the flow of rivers and capture silt and sediment, depriving farmers downriver of their benefits.

River Ganges

These Indian Hindu women are bathing in the Ganges River, a sacred act in their religion. This important river rises at the Gangotri glacier in the Himalayas and empties into the ocean in the Bay of Bengal.

people to grow crops and feed a large population. A similar situation existed in ancient Mesopotamia (modern Iran and Iraq) along the River Euphrates, as well as on the banks of the Indus River in Pakistan, the Ganges River in India and Bangladesh, and the Mekong River in Southeast Asia. Slowly, as farmers in these areas harvested more and more food, other people were freed from the need to work in agriculture. More time could be devoted to military conquest, architecture, science, philosophy, and music.

Rivers and Wildlife

Rivers provide a fantastic habitat for animals and plants. The Amazon River in South America, for example, has more than 2,000 species of fish living in it. Animals also live along the banks of rivers, dividing their time between the watery world and dry land. These animals include amphibians, such as frogs and toads; mammals, such as otters, water rats, voles, and beavers; and reptiles, such as snakes, crocodiles, and alligators. Trees, such as willows and alders, are adapted to the wet habitat and often crowd the banks of rivers.

All forms of life, plant or animal, are specially adapted to the particular environment in which they live. For example, beavers have learned how to build dams and alter rivers to suit their needs. They create a pond behind their dam about 65 to 100 feet (20–30 m) across and build a home called a lodge in the middle of it. Salmon are born in the upper parts of rivers. Once able, they swim out to sea. When the time comes for them to breed, they find the river in which they were born and swim back up it. Insects use rivers in their natural breeding cycle. Many water birds use rivers and lakes to build nests to rear their young. Migrating birds also use such areas of water as natural resting places en route from their summer breeding grounds to the regions where they spend the winter. Hunting birds that have adapted to life around rivers and lakes include the osprey and fish eagle. They hunt by swooping

Alaskan Salmon

Salmon returning from the sea to the rivers in which they were born, leaping up a waterfall. Once they reach the upper reaches of the river, they will breed.

River Dipper

The dipper, a river-dwelling bird found in America, Europe, and Asia. Dippers hunt in fast-flowing water by running along the riverbed.

Bengal Fishermen

Bangladeshi fishermen in the Bay of Bengal (opposite). Many rivers empty into this huge region, including the Ganges River and the Brahmaputra.

down to the water's surface and snatching out a fish with their long, sharp talons. One amazing little bird that haunts the banks of fast-flowing rivers in North America, Europe, and parts of Asia is called the dipper. It catches its meal of insect larvae by diving into rivers and actually swimming underwater along the bottom, using its bill to scoop up bugs.

Plants as Pollution Indicators

Plants have also adapted to rivers, and they often can tell us how healthy and clean—or how dirty and polluted—waterways are. For example, too much algae on a lake may mean that there are too many nutrients in the water. This generally means that fertilizer from local farms has gotten into the water through rivers that run into the lake or through the area's groundwater and have enriched it too much. This is bad for the environment. Algae grow very quickly and crowd out other plants. This creates problems for animals that feed on the plants, affecting the area's whole food chain.

Bangladesh—Land of Two Rivers

Bangladesh is located in southern Asia and is mostly surrounded by its large neighbor, India. It is home to more than 170 million people. Two of the greatest rivers in the world—the Ganges and the Brahmaputra—meet up in the middle of the country and flow out to the Indian Ocean. Their estuary at the Bay of Bengal is the largest in the world. Much of the country is made up of land in and around this huge delta. About three-quarters of the land is low-lying—about 10 feet (3 m) above sea level—and very flat. The people are mainly farmers, and the soil is rich. The staple crop is rice, but vegetables, tropical fruits, and beans are also grown extensively. Fish is another major source of food and income. More than one million tons (907,000 t) of fish are caught annually in the region.

The land is prone to extensive flooding during the monsoon season—from April to September. Annual rainfall totals about eight and a quarter feet (2.5 m), and most of it falls during this season. The many people that live and farm on the fertile plains are annually at risk. The natural flooding cycle has been made worse by human activity. For example, people have cut down stretches of the mangrove swamps that provide some protection from the ocean's waves and hurricane winds. In addition, in the Himalayan Mountains to the north, trees have been cut down. This has led to even more flooding when the snows melt and swell the rivers. Trees help to retain water, and without them, the water runs off very fast into the rivers, which then speed down to the lowlands, where they flood. People prepare for these hard times every year. Even so, in bad years, many people are drowned, houses are swept away, and farms are ruined. There is a very real concern that if global warming affects the level of the seas and oceans around the world, most of this wetland country could be permanently underwater.

Rivers and Wetlands in Danger

About half of the world's wetlands have been filled in, drained, or otherwise changed by human intervention over hundreds of years. Most of this has happened in the northern hemisphere in the developed countries of North America and Europe. It is a reflection of people's power to alter the environment to suit their needs. It is also a reflection of people's attitudes toward wetlands—regions of bog, fen, marsh, and swamp have mostly been seen as wasteland. They do not produce anything of obvious benefit to humans, so they have been changed into useable land or exploited for their water resources. Of the wetlands that do remain, many are affected by pollution or by nonnative species that have been introduced into their waters.

Drainage

The main reason wetlands have been drained is to dry out the land so it can be used for economically productive activities, such as growing crops, grazing cattle, and building houses or businesses. Scientists have estimated that about 80 percent of all wetland habitat loss has been due to drainage for agriculture. In many cases, reeds, sedges, and bulrushes have been swapped for wheat, corn, and vegetables. This is a movement away from biodiversity.

A thousand years ago, the inhabitants of what is today the Netherlands started to drain their saltwater and freshwater marshes. They called the reclaimed lands **polders**. The skill and expertise the Dutch gained over time from building dikes and canals to control the water and run it off was exported centuries later to countries such as England. The fens of Lincolnshire and Cambridgeshire in eastern England were drained and claimed as valuable farmland with the help of Dutch engineers in the 17th and 18th centuries. Today, salt marshes in North Carolina have been filled in with sand to create useful dry land, and Chicago, one of the largest cities in the U.S., is built on swampland that was once full of wildlife.

Draining wetland regions has a devastating effect on the animals and plants that depend entirely upon these habitats for their

Low-lying Landcapes

Windmills and man-made canals are typical of the low-lying landscape of the Netherlands. The people of this region became highly skilled at draining wetlands to create farmland.

Flooded Fens

A flooded fenland in eastern England. This landscape has been created from wetlands by constant draining over hundreds of years to produce fertile farmland.

survival. Draining or filling wetlands can also have a profound effect on such natural occurrences as flooding. Yet many wetlands around the world are in constant danger from the insatiable appetite of humans to develop landscapes for housing, farming, and other economic purposes.

Dams

Dams are built for good reasons. They can provide cheap energy for industries and homes through hydroelectric power generation. They can help control floodwaters during times of heavy rainfall. And they can provide a regular water supply to farmers for irrigating crops.

The Aswan High Dam was built in southern Egypt in the 1960s. It was an enormous project, involving 50,000 workers for more than 10 years. Today, it provides Egypt with up to 15 percent of its electricity needs. And because it allows farmers to have water on a regular basis for their crops, it has brought about a 25 percent increase in farm produce in some areas. These are all good things for local people.

However, the dam has also damaged some people's livelihoods and brought about other negative results. For example, the dam holds back a lot of the rich mud and sediment normally washed downstream by the Nile River. Because these natural fertilizers no longer reach some farmers' fields in the quantities they used to, the farmers have to use artificial fertilizers instead. This has had the unfortunate effect of increasing the levels of chemical pollution both on the land and in the river itself. Fishing around the estuary of the Nile and in the Mediterranean Sea has also suffered as a result of a decrease in the flow of water and an increase in polluting chemicals being carried downriver.

The Colorado River in the U.S. and Mexico is another major river that is seriously affected by dams—more than 1,000 of them, mostly in California. By the time the river reaches the Mexican border, the flow is very small compared to what it would be without the dams and irrigation channels that feed the deserts of southern California. Because there are two countries involved, the fact that America takes so much water from the Colorado River to help farmers grow fruit in the desert has become a contested political issue.

The Farakka **Barrage** in India was built over the Ganges River and has caused great problems in neighboring Bangladesh. Here, the amount of water flowing through the Ganges has gone down significantly. This has allowed the sea to push up into the delta of the river much farther than it could before, bringing its salt with it. The extra salt in the water has damaged farmland, made fresh water undrinkable, and harmed the freshwater fishing industry.

Largest Dam

The Itaipu Dam on the Parana River in Brazil, the largest dam in the world, was built to provide the region with hydroelectric power. More than 90 percent of Brazil's electricity comes from harnessing the energy of its rivers in this way.

Taking Fresh Water

In many parts of the world, water is scarce. This includes the countries of the Middle East and the Persian Gulf—parts of Turkey, Syria, Jordan, Iran, Iraq, and Israel; Africa—Egypt, Algeria, Libya, and the Sudan; Europe—around the Mediterranean in countries such as Greece, Italy, France, and Spain; Australia; and the southwest coast of the U.S. In such places, water is a **commodity** that has a high price. Rivers and wetlands are often seen as a source of this precious commodity—not as places to be protected, but places to be exploited. Countries lucky enough to have a major river flow through otherwise dry land often divert the water to irrigate crops and provide water for homes and industry.

In some coastal wetlands, problems have been caused by people taking too much water from rivers that flow into them. For example, the Everglades in Florida gets it water from Lake Okeechobee and the Kissimmee River. However, over a century of

Rio Grande

The Rio Grande following through the heavily farmed landscape of New Mexico. This river is under serious threat due to overuse of its water by the human population dependent upon it.

human activity, lots of canals, dikes, and levees have been built to harness this water for agriculture, homes, and industry in the region. As a result, habitats have been dried out and lost and fresh water has been made saltier because so much of it has been pumped away. This interferes with the breeding and feeding cycle of water birds that rely on the Everglades and can kill off the plants and trees that are not adapted to such high quantities of salt. Concentrations of chemicals such as mercury have also been found in the alligators and other big predators of the region, due to concentrations building up in the water and the food chains.

A similar situation has occurred along the Murray River in Australia. Here, water has been taken from the river to irrigate local crops, which has caused a buildup of salts washed into the water. Trees that grow on the floodplain have died because of the extra-salty water that washes over their roots in times of flood.

Murray River

The Murray, Australia's second-longest river, is under threat of salting up and drying out because too much water is taken from it by people needing to water their crops and animals.

Pollution of Rivers and Lakes

Great rivers and lakes everywhere have been polluted. Lakes Michigan, Erie, and Ontario, for example, have on their shores some of the largest cities and biggest industries in America and

Canada. Throughout the 1950s and 1960s, when industry was growing rapidly, the lakes were heavily polluted. Lake Erie was once declared dead because it had so little fish and plant life left. Fortunately, the situation has changed. Under pressure from local people, governments passed laws and regulations to clean up the lakes and neighboring rivers. Industries were forced to reduce pollution, and sewage treatment plants were upgraded as well. This has led to a return of native plants and freshwater fish to Lake Erie. The situation is today regularly monitored for changes in pollution levels.

Draining Wetlands

Pollution of waterways from industry and homes is a worldwide problem. Drainage into rivers and wetlands can concentrate toxins and destroy habitats.

Introduced Species

In some wetlands, species from other environments have been introduced into the **ecosystem**, causing problems for the wetland's native species. For example, the freshwater signal crayfish was brought to Britain to be farmed as a food source. It escaped into the rivers and wetlands of Britain and has since been taking over the habitat, causing the numbers of native

white-clawed crayfish to decline. The introduction of mink has brought about similar changes to these habitats, threatening such species as the water vole.

Imported Threat

The signal crayfish was introduced to the waterways of Britain from America. It threatens the native white-clawed crayfish, as well as native freshwater fish.

Rivers of Fire

In the past, some rivers became so polluted with chemicals from industries that they caught fire. This happened on the Cuyahoga River in Ohio in 1969. Today, many governments around the world have strict laws protecting waterways from raw sewage and chemicals. Companies caught polluting rivers and wetlands are fined large sums of money. Such action is one way in which society can help protect water resources. However, it is one thing to have a law that enables society to make these fines and another to have people monitoring the rivers and catching offenders.

The Future for Wetlands and Rivers

It is in the best interest of people everywhere to protect rivers and wetlands. Development must somehow be balanced with the need to look after these fragile habitats. This means finding ways to protect endangered sites around the world, reduce pollution from industry and homes, and use energy more efficiently in all areas of our lives.

What Is Sustainable Development?

Sustainable development is the key to the future of our rivers and wetlands. This means that people develop land economically to meet their needs and improve their lives, but not at the expense of the environment. Such development requires careful planning in terms of how we use rivers and wetlands and how we preserve them. In many cases, this may involve looking to native communities for examples. The native Australians have lived for 50,000 years on one of the driest continents on Earth. They thrived by planning their activities around the natural cycles of drought and rainfall. Similar situations can be seen in Africa, Asia, and South America, where traditional communities learned how to get the most out of natural cycles of flood and drought. They grew their rice in times of high water and harvested the crop when the waters went down. They fished when the rivers and coasts had an abundance and preserved the stocks for later when numbers decreased. These are examples of sustainable use of rivers and wetlands.

Protection and Preservation—Ramsar

In 1971, scientists and environmentalists from all over the world met in the Iranian city of Ramsar on the shores of the Caspian Sea to discuss how best to protect the world's wetlands from further drainage and pollution. First, the scientists involved in the convention had to define what was meant by the term wetland. They came up with the following definition: "Areas of marsh, fen, peatland, or water, whether natural or artificial, permanent or temporary, with water that is static or flowing, fresh, **brackish**, or salt." They then had to figure out a way to get countries all over the world to understand the importance of saving wetlands. They designated wetlands of great importance "Ramsar Sites," and these became protected areas. Their success can be measured by the fact that 138 countries have signed the convention treaty, which sets out the criteria for protecting world wetland sites, and more than 1,300 wetlands around the world have been designated Ramsar sites. This adds up to almost 300 million acres (121 million ha) of protected habitat.

Traditional Lifestyles

A native Australian hunting in a small creek in the Outback. These people have lived with nature, not against it, for thousands of years, protecting the landscape.

One of the most lasting achievements of this convention was simply raising concerns about wetlands and rivers in the minds of people around the world. It put these fragile places on the international stage and publicly explained that governments need to work together to save them.

Protected Sites

A Ramsar site in Somerset, England. There are now more than 1,500 such sites worldwide, protecting wetlands for future generations.

Ramsar Sites

Wetland and river sites protected by the Ramsar treaty are of great importance, not just for the country in which they are located, but for mankind as a whole. Although they range in size from tens of thousands of acres to just a few hundred, all have been judged to be internationally important. The governments of each of the countries in which the sites are found have given them at least some measure of protection from further exploitation. Here is a list of a few of the sites on the Ramsar list:

- The Everglades, Florida—1.5 million acres (607,000 ha)
- Izembek Lagoon National Wildlife Refuge, Alaska—416,000 acres (168,400 ha)
- Parque Nacional de Doñana, Andalucía, Spain—125,300 acres (50,700 ha)
- Upper Solway Flats and Marshes, Scotland—75,900 acres (30,700 ha)
- Strangford Loch, Northern Ireland—38,500 acres (15,600 ha)
- Rannoch Moor, Scotland—3,700 acres (1,500 ha)
- Llyn Idwal, Wales—35 acres (14 ha)
- The Sundarbans, Bangladesh—1.5 million acres (607,000 ha)
- The Okavango Delta, Botswana—17 million acres (6.9 million ha)

Artificial Wetlands

In many areas, people have created **reservoirs** and artificial lakes. These bodies of water can have a double benefit. They can collect water needed by local communities for drinking, washing, and industry. They can also create havens for wildlife and water-loving plants. A number of artificial lakes were dug out and dammed in Wales to supply the growing water needs of large cities and towns. However, in some cases, people who lived in small villages in valleys that were due to be flooded forever in order to create the reservoirs had to move from their homes. They were compensated for this by the government. Many myths and legends have grown up around these drowned villages. It is said, for example, that you can hear the ghostly sound of church bells still ringing from beneath the waters of one artificial lake. In times of very bad drought, the lakes sometimes dry up so much that people can see some of the old buildings emerging from the low waters.

Man-made Wetlands

The Shasta reservoir in northern California is a lake created when the Sacramento River was dammed. This artificial wetland has become an important habitat in the region.

Tourism and Wetlands

In today's highly mobile world, people choose many different types of vacations to suit their tastes. Two growing types of vacations are what have been called **eco-tourism** and adventure tourism. Wetlands can provide adventurous individuals who like wild places, animals, and plant life with a fantastic vacation destination. Travel agencies have recognized that there is money to be made from organizing bird-watching events, for example. Wetlands provide breeding and feeding grounds for migrating birds all over the world. Many people enjoy seeing the rare birds that gather at certain times of the year.

The North American Waterfowl Management Plan

Waterfowl are birds that live in wetlands, such as ducks and geese. Because wetlands have shrunk in size, these birds have been reduced in number. The countries of Canada, the U.S., and Mexico have collectively tried to do something about this in North America. They have made a management plan that includes preserving the birds' homes and breeding sites across the continent. The management plan is being carried out through local and regional actions. A big part of the plan's goal is to educate people and involve communities and schools in helping out—for example, by recording bird populations in their area.

Wildfowl Crossing

A Canadian goose with its goslings. Geese and other water birds suffer when their habitats are taken from them.

This type of exploitation of wetlands is perhaps ideal. It brings in money that can be directly attributed to the existence of the wetland. If carefully and sensitively managed, it also causes very little disruption to the life of the animals being observed or to the natural habitat as a whole.

Tourist Attraction

Adventurous tourists kayaking on the Kickapoo River in Wisconsin. Named after a tribe of Native Americans, this river today provides recreation for local people and visitors.

Saving Peat Bogs

Peat bogs are a valuable habitat found in Russia, Finland, Denmark, Ireland, Scotland, Wales, England, and Canada. They have been used by people for thousands of years as a source of fuel. The peat is dug up and dried. It can then be burned on an open fire, providing warmth and a means of cooking food. Because peat bogs have been overused, they have been shrinking in size around the world. On average, peat is formed naturally at a rate of about three and a third tons (3 t) per acre (0.4 ha) every year. If people use peat at a greater rate than this, the result will be a continual shrinking of the habitat. Apart from the loss of this rare and declining habitat, burning peat releases carbon dioxide into the atmosphere. This adds to global warming.

*Today, peat is more frequently used for garden **compost** than for heating homes. This practice has come under attack from environmentalists, and more people have turned to other types of compost garden fertilizer. One of the largest peat bogs in Britain was bought in 1990 by the Nature Conservancy Council to protect it from further exploitation.*

Conservation Organizations

Wetlands are one of the world's great natural habitats. Like all other types of habitats, they have been reduced in size over hundreds of years as people have built more farms, hydroelectric power stations, houses, and factories. There are today dozens of organizations dedicated to protecting what remains of the world's wetlands. They spend millions of dollars every year trying to do so. Some of the well-known organizations fighting for life in natural habitats, including wetlands, around the world include:

• **Friends of the Earth**   www.foe.org
Founded in 1971 in Britain, Friends of the Earth is now one of the world's best-known and most respected environmental pressure groups.
• **World Wide Fund for Nature (WWF)**   www.panda.org
Founded in 1961, this Swiss-based organization raises money to fund conservation operations around the world, focusing in particular on endangered animals.
• **Greenpeace**   www.greenpeace.org/usa/
Founded in 1971 in Canada, Greenpeace has grown to become one of the world's biggest and most influential environmental pressure groups. It campaigns all over the world on behalf of the environment.
• **International Union for the Conservation of Nature (IUCN)**   www.iucn.org
This organization publishes *The Red Book*, which presents the most comprehensive picture we have today of the state of the planet in terms of threats to species.

What You Can Do to Help

In the fight to save our rivers and wetland habitats, we all have a role to play. We can all help to keep our planet healthy. The environment that it nurtures gives all living things what they need—food, water, light, and shelter. It is important for us and for future generations that it is able to continue to do so. Here are some ways you can help:

• Eat organic foods. These foods are not grown using pesticides and artificial fertilizers, which can contain chemicals that pollute waterways. Encouraging farmers to reduce pollution is a key step in protecting our precious habitats.
• Use less water. Take short showers rather than baths and put a brick in the tank of the toilet so that less water is used each time it is flushed. Fix dripping faucets as soon as possible, and report leaks in pipes. Rain barrels in gardens can collect rainwater for plants and vegetables instead of using water from the faucet.

• Avoid polluting water sources. Using **biodegradable** dishwashing liquids and laundry detergents will help.

• At school, try to learn as much as you can about your local waterways and wetland habitats. Visit a nearby nature reserve to learn about the wildlife and plants that depend on the habitat.

• Your school may have projects concerning local special habitats. Many schools around the world have been involved in helping to restore wetland habitats by cleaning them up—removing things that have been dumped in them, for example. You may be able to find out about such programs by checking out school Web sites.

Further Reading

Dugan, Patrick, ed. *Wetlands in Danger: A World Conservation Atlas*. New York: Oxford University Press, 1993.

Johnson, Rebecca L. *A Journey into a Wetland*. Minneapolis: Carolrhoda Books, 2004.

Reid, Greg. *Wetlands*. Philadelphia: Chelsea Clubhouse, 2003.

Rotter, Charles. *Wetlands: A Vanishing Resource*. Mankato, Minn.: Creative Education, 2001.

Stewart, Melissa. *Life in a Wetland*. Minneapolis: Lerner Publications, 2003.

Wallace, Marianne D. *America's Wetlands: Guide to Plants and Animals*. Golden, Colo.: Fulcrum, 2004.

Web sites

National Parks Conservation Association—Wetlands
http://www.npca.org/marine_and_coastal/wetlands

National Wilderness Institute
http://www.nwi.org

Sierra Club—Wetlands
http://www.sierraclub.org/wetlands/factsheets

U.S. Environmental Protection Agency—Wetlands
http://www.epa.gov/owow/wetlands

Wetlands International
http://www.wetlands.org

Glossary

Algae   A large and very diverse group of simple plants, ranging from single-celled organisms to enormous seaweeds. Algae are found both on land and in the water.

Barrage   A dam placed in a waterway to increase the depth of the water or to divert it into a channel for navigation or irrigation.

Biodiversity   The numbers and types of different plants and animals living in a specific environment.

Biodegradable   Something that can be broken down by bacteria or fungi. Non-biodegradable substances, such as many plastics and heavy metals, are very difficult to get rid of in an environmentally friendly way.

Brackish   Salty. Brackish water is not drinkable due to its high salt content.

Carbon   An element found in several forms and in combination with other elements to form compounds; combined with oxygen, it forms carbon dioxide. All living things have carbon in them.

Commodity   Something that is made for sale and profit.

Compost   Natural organic matter (leaves or other garden or kitchen waste, for example) that through a process of decomposition breaks down to form useful nutrients that can be recycled.

Delta   A triangular deposit of soil at the mouth of a river.

Ecology   The study of living organisms and their relationships with the environment.

Ecosystem   A natural unit of the environment in which all of the plants, animals, and nonliving components depend on each other in complex ways.

Eco-tourism   Tourism based upon a more sensitive approach to the impact that travelers have upon the landscapes they visit.

Estuaries   Places where rivers meet the sea, often called mouths of rivers. An estuary is usually defined as the area that is influenced by the tides coming in from and retreating back out to the sea.

Evolved   Scientists believe that life on Earth has developed, or evolved, over billions of years. The theory of evolution claims that all life has come from single-celled forms and has slowly become more complex.

Global warming   The process by which Earth's climate is thought to be getting warmer through an increase in greenhouse gases.

Greenhouse gases   Gases, including carbon dioxide and methane, that trap heat in Earth's atmosphere.

Habitats   Parts of an environment that are self-contained, supplying the needs of the organisms that live within them.

Hydroelectric power   Power produced by using the force and energy from moving water, such as a large river that has been dammed.

Insecticides   Chemicals used to stop insects from eating crops.

Irrigation   The taking of water from natural rivers, lakes, and rainfall to use on crops—for example, by building special channels along which the water can flow into fields.

Lagoons   Shallow, often salty lakes that are usually found close to the sea.

Marginalized   A word used to describe people, whole communities, nations, or tribes that have been pushed to the sidelines and not allowed to have their voice heard.

Monsoon   A wind that blows at certain times of the year in regions of southern Asia and brings huge quantities of rain. The regular rainy period in tropical countries is often called the monsoon season.

Mosses   Plants that do not have any flowers. There are more than 10,000 different species around the world.

Neutralizing   Making less harmful. The water hyacinth does this to potentially hazardous chemicals, providing a very useful function in cleansing the water in its vicinity.

Oasis   An area where water is found in an otherwise desert landscape. An oasis is a small, fertile place where animals, plants, and people live. (The plural is oases.)

Polders   Infertile coastal lands at or below sea level that have been saved from the sea and made useable for farmers by building dykes and other defenses.

Reservoirs   Places where water collects and is stored. Usually the word is used of an artificial lake built by people to provide towns and cities with a constant and regular supply of water.

Sediment   Materials (such as small particles of rock and vegetation) that settle at the bottom of a river, lake, or sea.

Silt   Fine-grained sediment that is deposited by a river as it reaches flatter ground on its journey to the sea.

Spawning   Laying large numbers of eggs in the water. Fish and other sea animals spawn every year.

Sustainable   Something that can be carried out indefinitely into the future.

Temperate   A term used to describe a climate that is neither too hot nor too cold. Temperate zones are found halfway between the hot tropics and the cold poles.

Treaty   An agreement by two or more parties that is written down and becomes legally binding.

Tundra   Land close to or inside the Arctic Circle, where the layer of soil just below the surface is permanently frozen due to year-round low temperatures.

Water cycle   The natural cycle in which water evaporates from bodies of water and is given out from plants into the atmosphere. Here it eventually condenses again to form clouds and precipitation.

Index

DATE DUE
